Blue Pajamas

Blue Pajamas

Poems

STEPHEN CUSHMAN

Louisiana State University Press

Baton Rouge

1998

Designer: Melanie O'Quinn Samaha
Typeface: AGaramond
Printer and binder: Thomson-Shore, Inc.

Library of Congress Cataloging-in-Publication Data

Cushman, Stephen, 1956–
    Blue pajamas : poems / Stephen Cushman.
    p. cm.
    ISBN 0-8071-2302-1 (cloth : alk. paper). —ISBN 0-8071-2303-X
(paper : alk. paper)
    I. Title
PS3553.U745B58   1998
811'—dc21   98-18936
                                      CIP

Thanks to the editors of these journals for publishing the following poems, some in earlier versions: *Agni:* "Two Freeze to Death Despite Experience"; *American Literary Review:* "The Pledge Taken at Fitzgerald's Grave"; *Black Bear Review:* "Indian Moon Moth," "Plant Identification"; *Concho River Review:* "Heartmeadow Farm, Allegany, New York"; *Chattahoochee Review:* "The Copperhead Vents in a Heat Wave"; *descant:* "Laundry by Hand"; *Florida Review:* "Farewell and Hail"; *Half Tones to Jubilee:* "Communion"; *Jeopardy:* "Grandfather, 1944," "Imposition of Ashes"; *Madison Review:* "One Comet at Bedtime"; *Mangrove:* "On Castrating the Dog"; *Maryland Review:* "Observation Deck," "Thoreau's Cairn"; *96 Inc:* "In Him There Is No Darkness at All"; *Poem:* "'War, Effect of a Shell on a Confederate Soldier'"; *Poet Lore:* "Adoration," "Invidia"; *Raritan:* "Diet"; *Rockford Review:* "Old Perithia"; *Shenandoah:* "Rapunzel"; *Southern Review:* "Except I Shall See"; *Southwest Review:* "Boy on Horseback"; *Timbuktu:* "At the London Zoo," "Blood and Snow," "Just the End of Time," "Therapy"; *Virginia Quarterly Review:* "The Kingdom of Things"; *Walden Review:* "Blue Pajamas," "Fling Island."

Thanks also to Charles, George, Greg, and Mary Lee; to David Slavitt, who read the manuscript for LSU Press; to John Easterly, who edited it; and to Sandra, who sifted every one.

To the three with whom I make one

Contents

1

Except I Shall See

2

Thoreau's Cairn

3

Heartmeadow Farm

1

Except I Shall See

Black-maned, black-tailed, a gray horse stands
tied to a locust tree outside St. Thomas.
Inside, in the usual pew, his white-haired master
bows his head as the organ plays Brahms,
"My Heart Abounds with Joy," but hard as he prays
he cannot dodge the image of a farmboy,
shot in the cheek or the groin,
laid in that pew after Cedar Mountain
or Chancellorsville, the house of the Lord
become the house of chloroform and amputation.

Winter sky the color of the horse
with small feet, delicate ears, quick eye
curls over the brick church as the man prays
that his mind might quiet, might free itself
from the hobble of loss, from remorse
that he ordered Pickett on, might somehow escape
the distraction of the farmboy or the sense
that all around him the mahogany pews
with cushioned kneeling-bars, racks
of red hymnals, black Books of Common Prayer,
begin to hum with the passion of the wounded
rising out of the groan-logged wood

as I pray now that the plaque on his pew
across the aisle, or the one by the locust tree
where the gray horse waited, not just lift
my heart to history and strand it there,
abandoned to annals, but reveal to me in worldliness
the world without end, for if I cannot come to Thee
through thoughts of another man on his knees,
I doubt that I can come at all.

Bodies make good business, Gardner knew
after his Antietam show took the North
and sealed the break with Brady.
But the long hiatus of losses that followed
meant those with the cameras and chemicals
couldn't get at the damn battlefields.
He sat in the capital and stewed into summer
till Pennsylvania started brewing and a chance
to scoop his old boss, that bastard,
sent him moving the wagons through Maryland
so fast he bumped into Stuart at Emmitsburg.
Detained, questioned, released, he slogged
the last muddy miles, lucky to reach
Rose's farm before the burial detail.

Thirty-four Georgians from Semmes's brigade
laid out by their buddies for burial
but abandoned. After three days
of decomposing Gardner, Gibson, O'Sullivan
found them fattened by gasses but otherwise
neatly arranged in rows around the field
on their backs, their features intact
except for those odd O's the mouths shape
when jaws go slack and lips stretched tight
by bloating cheeks make faces of men
who've stuffed themselves at a picnic
and before nodding off for naps in the sun
amuse themselves with minstrel routines.
At least they have each other, all together

except for one who would have spoiled the fun,
his belly blown away, the camera angle
asking us into his thorax. O'Sullivan shot
the eight-by-ten, Gardner the stereo
the War Photograph and Exhibition Company
of Hartford, Connecticut, would market
to collectors with a blurb beginning
"This poor fellow" and closing with
"A Word as to Prices." But first they placed

a shell on the ground above the right knee
and laid a rifle across both legs, the same gun
they propped by the Devil's Den Sharpshooter,
those bastards. In the right foreground
a severed left hand gropes toward the trigger.

Clumps of dried peppers, onions, corn
dangle from rafters blackened by smoke.
In one corner stands a hand-carved chest.
Against the wall a double bed
twitches with fleas. Remains
of pigmeat, crackers, red wine
mix with maps in light from a can
of burning gasoline.

Outside the farmhouse,
burnt, golden fields of Tunisia,
dry, starry nights in Sicily,
vanish into November in Italy,
into a cold of flooded roads and fields
emerald green with winter wheat.

Does Ohio give a holy God
damn about Anzio, or an eight-year-old
girl care that her father's revered
by wet, shivering, unshaven men
still alive to take his orders?

She includes him in her prayers;
he includes her in his letter
home in June, finished the night
German shells smash this scene

and the two years of his absence
set out to age with her
aging, to give her voice
its fluted tone, her moods
their silver shade, as she chooses to marry
a man not at all like him and mothers
a son who sucks loss with her milk.

Gardenia

No longer the smell of a flower but the smell
of light seeping through blinds
onto the page my father is reading. For him,
it may be the smell of the page or the spiced
smell of the words themselves, read at the foot
of the bed. For my sister at the head,
it may be the smell of her page or the jasmine
smell of her own hair, as she dreams
about China and someone to give flowers.

Someone has sent flowers. Outside,
it's February in the tough part of town,
and someone has sent flowers to fill the small room
with the smell of the bandage that wraps
half the head, of the iodine stain by the bridge
of the nose, of the blue, blue eye she no longer has.

No longer the smell of a flower but the smell
of her sleeping as, the other two reading,
one tear depends from the widowed eye's lash,
heavy with light and the smell of some Asia
where a shined tear still drops, she wakes,
and I feel the long squeeze of her hand.

Whoever invented Mother's Day
never thought of mine, every few years
the second Sunday in May lighting on
that anniversary. Infant mortality.
What a phrase. How the Latin pacifies
a fussy runt into abstraction
with fat linguistic nipples speakers
of English can suck themselves stupid on,
lost in thoughtless bliss unnicked by pictures
of my mother, wounded at twenty-two,
too much to drink, straying out through
Ohio cornfields, a midwestern Ophelia
dwarfed by the stalks, chanting back
at blackbirds as the family hunted.

What card should I send from the racks
of saccharine pap and clever drivel
commemoration can be reduced to?
No greeting voices the feeling
a cold spring leaks into the temperate
lake of my life each time I float
over this day or speaks of the space
that gapes between me and the later
sister who lived; no message makes
family attachments half as attractive
as monastic withdrawal, one more temptation
the fear of losing leads us into, or says
that she showed me how to give up
a father, child, eye and still defy.

The salve my mother smeared my skin
with smelt like tar. Something hidden,
erupting through this organ
bones and blood come wrapped in,
found my knees the place to begin
its awful visitation,
the itching rash which brands me kin
to Job. Even after he'd been
flayed with loathsome sores by Satan,
his lips refused to curse and sin
by cursing. With a shard of broken
pot he sat down to scrape his skin.
I'm not claiming that a fallen
angel betting against God's the engine
behind each scaly lesion.
Still, like copperhead or moccasin,
I'd slough, if I had the option,
shedding what returns again
and again unasked, an irritation
made maddening by its repetition.
But my skin and I come twin;
what's under it must redden
this raw script upon that skin
until the record has been written.

Invidia

Of the seven she's the deadliest.
Goltzius must have thought so, too,
giving her biceps, triceps, abdominals
corrugated like a body-builder's.
With a snake for a sash, her tunic
hangs from her waist, her breasts
flabby sacks nobody sucks. For hair
she has a turban of serpents,
for belongings a bouquet of snakes
in her left hand, in her right
a heart she's about to bite into.

Of the seven she's the deadliest.
Goltzius must have thought so, too,
when, arriving at her eyes, he left them
vacant ovens, the underlid flesh
sagging away, exposing smooth bone.
Worst of all, she's half-smiling

at her six sisters, more human
than she, if pathetic and silly:
the proud one with her precious mirror,
the fat one with her eating disorder,
the one who can't keep her clothes on
her body or her hands off herself,
another in a helmet having a tantrum,
another lugging her life-savings,
the wonderful slow one, a snail on her
shoulder, too lazy to button her blouse;

or at Goltzius, whose core she holds
to her mouth, a heart she must have hounded
more than her sisters to wring from him
a likeness so little like theirs; or at me,
poor sinner, woozy with her poison,
witched by his venomous image of envy
into an image of envy.

But we who had none survived
the same conditions, winds gusting
a hundred, windchill seventy below,
visibility ninety-five feet.
Beer we brought for the summit
froze into bricks. Slowed by air
so fierce it held us if we fell,
we picked our way from cairn to cairn
over the featureless tableland,
a schoolteacher and three boys who'd read
several good books about mountains.
Losing a mitten meant losing a hand.
I shouldn't be alive today.

Twenty years later what have I got?
A pink carbon of weather data
pressed in a dictionary against the page
with *mountain* on it; yesterday's paper
reporting how rescuers found
two bodies huddled in a gully;
and the familiar feeling I'm unfamiliar
with what I feel. Pride we made
no mistakes? Guilt for luck
we didn't deserve? Gratitude the peak
that smothered them suffered us?
Or mostly fear a piece of me
didn't pull through

the growl of wind, the clawing cold,
the smell and taste of wool and snow
filling the eyes with only a face
wrapped in white, turning away
from something inside that didn't survive
and looks for these, its resurrections?

Communion

Drink this. I sip and taste
the lips this cup has touched,
bitten, split, lips

now peeled away that barely
brushed here near the end,
brisk lips pressed on their way

to or from delicious lips,
widowed lips, lips someone
deaf has read, stumbling

lips that move during reading,
nimble lips that snip off words,
lips puckered with pain

of the body, the migraine,
back spasm, menstrual cramp,
or, unabating, not of the body.

Shed for thee. White cloth
wipes my germs from the rim,
but do one or two slip through,

communicating themselves to
the next at the rail and the next?
Why else do we come, contagious

and susceptible, but to catch
whatever's going around
and pass it on?

Seventh Sunday after the Epiphany
and one verse into "I Want to Walk as a Child"
the old organ calls it quits, struck dumb
as Zechariah, leaving congregation and choir
to go it alone through the desert extending
from epistle to gospel, Corinthians to Luke.

Pretty clever of the new Rector. Must be
some strategy he learned in seminary,
like the slap of a Zen master, to jolt
the faithful from liturgical complacency
into Protestant satori. But the organist
flusters too much for one in cahoots,

and it's no simulation but a vision come true
from the den of nightmares dreamed repeatedly
near the end of summer before school resumes
like the ones about walking onstage to perform
music unpracticed or lines unlearned
or both with no clothes. How blushingly naked

our voices feel, especially the raw baritone
I usually fake it with, skulking around
the organ's low notes. For heaven's sake
get me out of here before the panic
that erupts when structure dissolves
washes me under. But from the pew behind,

calm and sturdy, steady as a star
that burns through the worst hour of night,
a clear soprano never falters,
never stumbles under the added burden or betrays
the least doubt that we were always meant to sing
this way, accompanied only by each other

in the manner of the chapel when the creed
was young, long before my struggle to trust
in letting go and leaning on an unseen
source of courage as I steer by her
back to my place in our resolute hymning
of haphazard lapses that connect us like hyphens.

Imposition of Ashes

I've fussed enough with faith.
Do I trust in things unseen?
We've discussed all this before.

Smash the crust of clever answers.
Let's get down to what must
be justified: clumps of dust

collect in closets, over tables,
under couches, the gray fur
houses grow, unless one skins

with mop and rag. But why?
Dust isn't so disgusting
if I sit where I can see it

swim in the sun, each flake
a distant cousin to claim as kin
at the moonlit reunion when I return.

Whitman would have learned a word
for the things she holds in her hands,
the nomenclature from the manual
or a scrap of slang coined by pilots
nosing through bad fog or snow.

He would have learned her title, too,
a name for the occupation of standing
on a runway waving in the planes at night,
ear-guards outside her long brown hair
and nothing but two wands to guide
wings roaring with a heavenly sound

as of a rushing mighty wind
filling the house apostles sat in
when the cloven tongues came down,
orange and glowing, like the things
she holds in her hands, sketching perfect
circles, exes, arcs against the dark
in a language I do not know
but in this moment understand.

And Whitman, dead a hundred years,
would have apostrophized the figures
of O this athletic woman, O these
magnificent machines, though deviled
by doubts about power descending
over blue mountains without spirit,

but I, with a hundred years to grow
used to its absence, stand deafened
in unexpected excess and plenitude.

Its name is Myrtiotissa.
—Lawrence Durrell, *Prospero's Cell*

Our Lady of the Myrtles kneels beside
the olive hem of Agios Georgios,
Her whitewashed belfry a cool fleck
against green flanks of mountain, its summit
humped like a wave about to swamp
the cliff-backed beach of khaki sand
a thousand cloudless feet below.

Floating in the sea, one looks up
to cliffs with craters, divots, pits
like those in trunks of olive trees,
hollows the shape of niches in chapels
where icons sit protected by glass
the faithful kiss, leaving prints
that only show when the light tilts right

across the beach bathers go naked on,
some with buttocks as white as the monastery,
others with scarlet sunburns on theirs,
a few wholly without the ghosts of clothes,
their skin the uniform color of clove
as though they never felt their nakedness
roasting on the slow spit of paradise.

Old Perithia

If I dressed in white and took a vow
of silence, I couldn't keep it
better than old stone houses keep it here,
broken only by birdsong and sheepbells
faint as far-off wind chimes or by bees
vibrating a fully blossomed apple tree
whose petals clutter the cobblestones
and uncobbled streets gone back to grass.
But if dressed in white, I would stand out
against a purple moat of wild geraniums
surrounding one abandoned house that nests
in this high bowl at the heart of the massif,
the spiked summit of the Almighty breaching above
a ridge-cupped world where neighbors hug close
and traces of a wall still belt the village
against raiders and pirates. The old die,
the young go down to work for tourists
beside the sea, leaving behind the seven
churches that served the village, bells
in the belfries hung to ward off
the stillness of perpetual siesta,
one church to visit each day of each week
it takes to make a home of a ghost town.

Supplicants bent on raising the dead
tripped for three days in the sanctuary,
sealed from light in windowless rooms,
chewing hallucinogens. Their magic beans
don't appear in Homer, nor the bronze windlass
for mechanical trickery, nor the puny labyrinth
ruined in sunlight that when dark, intact,
bewildered the pilgrim into the underworld.

Who could fall for this fakery? Did the man
of many turnings, opening the throats
of black ram and ewe, wink at the joke,
go through the motions, humor the priests?
From the ruins one can trace across the plain
Acheron, a braid of poplar and willow
hardly wide enough for a ferry to ply
or passenger to fill the boatman's fist,

but who cares? On the stairs leading down
to the black House of Hades, unbelief
falters in the gloom of a chamber hewn
from solid rock beneath the sacred hall;
skepticism pines for the upper air,
for red poppies sprouting among the tumbled
blocks of the purification room, a place
to get a grip again, shake off the shivers,

expurgate all the faces, all the shades.

Diet

Places I've been stay with me.
Black wine, fresh in bottles without labels,
washing down lamb at the village saint's festival,
as children skip through piles of fire

and dancers link in a circling line,
makes for the recent fullness of my face;
and my belt won't tighten quite as far
now that I've climbed the highest mountain

to lounge all day with a monk up there,
sipping his brandy, watching the snow melt;
and because I let the lady at the market
mother me with olives, warm bread, white cheese

there's more of me than there used to be.
Some take pictures to help them remember.
I fatten, carting extra pounds through customs
with nothing to declare. But back in the gaze

of eyes left behind, it's clear my souvenirs must go.
I hate to lose; how much more I hate
to have to choose to lose all traces
of the faraway place one never says no.

If I were a nasty drunk tossing gold-flecked
wineglasses over the garden wall or writing
with lipstick on my hostess's gown, this
would be the place to promise true amendment.
If I lived on nothing but irony,
I'd gorge on his name, Francis Scott Key,
or the four-lane traffic of Rockville,
Maryland, laving the expatriate's
little Catholic churchyard. If I came here
a pilgrim to linger over the last sentence
of *Gatsby* engraved on his granite slab,
I'd weep for Daisy weeping over shirts.
But I'm only pinching mulberries
ripe on nearby bushes and renewing
before they drop, crush, stain the pavement
a vow I always vow that hereafter
in my godly, righteous, sober life
I'll find ways to misbehave, flap and roar.

2

Thoreau's Cairn

Marianne Moore, I love you.
True, your eye prefers the feline
  demeanor of the mind, its razor
    pupils, claws in hiding, stealthy purr,
while mine

inclines toward dogs with hanging
tongues, gregarious grins, trust in smell.
  Still, faced with the choice of seeing one
    big cat in captivity or none
at all,

you would never whine or fuss
beside the Wolf Wood, "What a shame
  to witness *canis lupus* taken
    out of context, his North American
domain

exchanged for this fenced yard in
Regent's Park with imitation
  den." I, too, dislike the outrage,
    our violation of arrangements
to cage

the specimen that can spawn
or breed beyond its habitat.
  But what's the alternative?
    To live, letting wolves and big cats live
their own

ways into oblivion,
never snatching a pup or cub
  to sniff the odors of London's air
    and bask in an artificial lair
through sub-

freezing nights? Picture this zoo,
all its creatures freed, the cages
  banging their doors in the sun; picture
    nothing captured in the glare of bare
pages.

The old cat, nineteen this September,
can't hold his kills the way he used to.
With chuckled coughs and gaggings, this gourmet
spills his guts, but only after spasm,
heave, convulsion enhance the appearance of
what he's done his damnedest to dismember.

This kind of thing is difficult to love,
especially when some shiny plasm
now decorates the dining room rug.
But today the mess differs. Paper towel
and sponge in hand, I see something moving,
survivor from the belly of the cat.

A baby something: mouse, possum, squirrel?
Not even baby, still tethered
by cord to jellied membrane, red-vesseled,
lifted clean from a gutted mother.
Beside it, gray, sister or brother, dead.
But it lives, pink with blood still pumping

through tiny features, soon-to-be eyes that
look like bruises, ears, and first cousins of
fingers. And its mouth, as though by clockwork,
opens and gropes, unused to air, maybe
a reflex for sucking it will never do,
its jaws jolted wide by what to it is pain.

Rather, soon-to-have-been eyes and the rest.
The cat has retired, unconcerned and smug.
What did you expect? he says. At my age
the only race I win is with expecting
females come to term. It's that or plunder
nests the moment they deliver. Don't rage

at me. I put the towel and sponge away.
All that afternoon the little mouth
went at inedible air. With evening
I moved it to the porch, seizures slowing,

and with my dinner napkin made its bed.
The rest was left to Maine coast August night,

to sharp stars and a northwest taste of frost.
No miracle was sought, no gods tempted
to descend and show me they could rescue.
The rest was left to what all odds are against:
in what is cool and sea-damp and adverse,
enough can be found to nourish and nurse.

Fling Island

On the chart a circle girdled with asterisks,
this island never visited
ringed by a necklace of ledges
guarding it like teeth ready to
puncture the wood-flesh of hulls.
At low tide we'd see them, but at high
they wait, wet, in the sea's cheek.
We can only come at high; last time
in this channel, rock and keel made
a noise I still hear when I close my eyes
to wonder how the end will sound.
But after the last buoy, a black can
off the point, not a single asterisk
swims into sight on the smooth, blank
tablet of water randomly dimpled
by wind? rain? fish? rocks? I, the only one
who doesn't wear glasses, am navigator
and haven't a clue whether the surface
I'm reading prints what's above or below.
We coast the last few yards, quiet and slow.

The island's only inhabitants, two
clammers last seen by the keeper
of Eagle light, set out in a blizzard
but never made the Saturday night dance
eighty years ago. The course home
takes the way they should have gone,
or did go, until the one wave so cold
spilled them out and stopped their hearts
inside the heavy clothes that dragged them under
the sunny surface we now skim. Drunk, burned,
relieved of charts by deeper water,
I squint into glare at a piece
of driftwood with ears that turns
to a deer a mile from the nearest shore.
Close up its eyes fill mine. Then we veer
off so as not to see the head disappear
and know it never made Fling Island or found
a way through the ring of ledges to rocky

beach, climbed the grassy fringe, pierced
the belt of spruce and raspberry brambles
to the island's core, an inner
field of fireweed and goldenrod, and curled up
to wait out the passing pink and yellow.

On Castrating the Dog

His last afternoon as himself
passes slowly. We sprawl in the grass
not speaking, he at the end of a chain
straining toward a distant bark,
hot to bolt, roam, cavort, I longing
to explain reasons for being the way
he'll be tomorrow. Two months ago the vet
cupped them in his palm ("Too small—still a pup")
as I do now, handling roundness no breast can hold
a candle to, as much a part of us, our shaping
mystery, as arrows or angularity.

Altered. Of available words it hurts
least, utters least of the gaping
wound I imagine or the shaved loins
of gray stubble and modest scar that appear
instead. When from beyond the pond
the farthest barking fills his ears
or an invisible bitch signals in the wind,
what has been cut from him becomes what he's cut
off from, a remote yelp or smell
almost arousing a partial remembrance
in the evening when the grass turns black
like his fur and the only light to see by
burns in the bodies of slow-blinking fireflies.

One Comet at Bedtime

Rid of the nuisance of light, my binoculars
dust the distance from faint stars,
wipe them shiny with discs of vision.
Shooting sparks from a meteor shower
streak the field, distracting, but this year
they aren't what I'm out after.
From the Great Square of Pegasus, lower
left corner, I float groping a few million miles
across a finger's width of starless void
to an unnamed trapezoid, then bear left again
and start to sweep the spine of Pisces.
Scouting east as far as Cetus, I track back
and there she blows, the promised smudge
with an English name. Rub my eyes, brush
the lens, fiddle with the focus, and still
in all that sharpness it stays a blur,
a single smear of breath on the deepest mirror
like breath I have tonight, my birthday,
but not in the year the comet returns.
Stiff-necked and frozen, I turn to earth
again and see the feeder, empty now
of titmice and chickadees, but the first place
I'll scan tomorrow for the juncos I love most,
eyes on the ground, pecking galaxies of seed.

Therapy

A sharp flap; wings brush my hair.
Five times in dim woods it dives for my head.
Face up to eyes swooping, I
chicken and duck.

A game of nerves for a summer night.
My first owl, small but fearless
silhouette on a poplar branch,
whinnies low notes

from its underworld throat.
Wing-grazed, scalped by feathers
in a hall of black leaves,
I should fear more

what beak and talons could
wreak on my face, should get my
flesh the hell out of the
cave dark woods become

into open fields where a little light lingers.

Indian Moon Moth

Pale green bow tie the size of a child's hand
you cling to my car door here in the parking lot
a night butterfly in the nosey light of day
having commuted fifty-five lashing miles an hour
from the cluttered little house that needs painting
on the cluttered little car that needs painting
to the job that gives me more to do faster
than it gives me more to spend a piece of last night
still stuck to me despite the toothbrush shower shave
despite the button-down and Windsor knot
a lovely piece with long tails on the hind wings
feathery antennae maroon markings the shape of snake heads
that rides with me in traffic through intersections
my mascot totem talisman familiar I could say
making more of you than I need to
since by day I belong to my skin income organs
my year of birth country of citizenship
but by night I belong to no one but you

sounds ho-hum compared to *Magicicada septendecim;*
yet it simplifies matters by finessing the prefix,
which coming from *meg-* would signify greatness

and make perfect sense for a nymphal nap
that lasts underground the time it takes us
to vacate the womb and conquer a driver's license.

But if *Magi* comes from *magh-,* it signifies power
that steams from holes they drill in the lawn
and exoskeletal husks that stick to our eaves

in memory of any Greek who carved their likeness
on the doorpost he wanted to shield from evil.
In that case, *magic, might,* and *machine* would all be

cousins, along with the wise men, and help to explain
the spell that's cast afternoons when the drone
keeps rising, bloating the air till it crests

as background music for attacks brought on
by looking too long at their red eyes divining
how lost I could be by the time they return.

I'm not just fangs and venom. I thirst too
and need shade from all excessive sun
can do to us whose bodies warm or cool
with seasonal whims. Give me one good reason
cold-blooded should mean unfeeling when it's we
who sense each degree thermometers inch
more keenly than any princess feels a pea.
Or take mean as a snake, snake in the grass,
snake pit; such phrases poison self-esteem.
As for my family, I'd sooner admit incest
than that I'm a viper. But I'm not lethal,
or rarely so compared to tropical cousins
who ferry angels on their tongues. Nor do I
hunt the fool who thrusts barehanded into brush
or wades through overgrown woods in July.
And I'm not vain, although I know my body
entrances people when they behold it
folded under a rainspout among the roses,
my cinnamon skin banded by russet bells
in an understated, earth-toned elegance
that will not lose composure faced with rudeness
ribbing me with sticks, as though I would ever
quit my sanctuary within the heart
of the hydrangea and venture forth to risk
chance encounters with constricting king snakes.

Polar cold petrifies the pond,
lacing up skates untouched for years,
the blades still blessed with teeth enough
to bite the perfect ice and hold
a sharp turn, sudden stop,
prolonged glide from bank to bank
as the sun hovers, making the pond
grunt and burp, or the moon serves
milk in its shallow bowl, or snow
sifts finely over this foreign land,
its mildness home now but a home
not without sickness for another
where frozen solids aren't so fleeting
and what's fluid flows with gratitude.

Enough's enough. I'm off to get high
in an oak on the ridge by a ladder
hunters have lashed to a platform
twenty feet skyward. What a view.
The hollow bottoms out a hundred yards below
the arches of my bootsoles and mountains
make blue barricades thirty miles away.
Thank goodness my fears do not include
the one of heights and motion sickness
rarely troubles me, even though
northwesterly gusts rough up the oak
so bad the deer stand bucks and plunges
in heavy seas that one of these days
will snap its weathered wood
out from under me and I will be done
with daring the wind and climbing back down.

I've strayed. Or has the tour left me
alone by the lake, the water clear
as gin or windows one forgets but
rediscovers in attempts to touch, whetting
edges of speckled stones like one
I pocket to free my hands for washing,
splashing, cupping a mouthful that magnifies
their palms, deepening my lifelines?

Something big with wings lights in a tree
behind the rectangle of granite posts
and cairn begun a hundred years ago.
Here a boulder wrestled by someone intent
on making his mark, there a pebble balanced
on the boulder to speak for the meek,
somewhere the stones of people I know
who've come in ones or twos and gone.

I add mine and advance to flush
the brooding thing with wings
that sails through the cedars
leaving me turning
thirty in the same spot he did,
alone by the water, rattled by love.

3

Heartmeadow Farm

Merton meditated in this meadow,
mountain-side valentine for the village below,
now owned by friends. Steep, treeless
slope of grass, the field funnels
to a point, its fringe of oaks
framing another, nether world: roads,
houses, a university. Beyond, a ring
of hills. So inclined, the eye
gets pulled up and down at once.
At the cleft between arcs, upper humps
of the heart, the loud blood of summer
dizzies; a falling feeling comes.
Is this the monk's tremendous mystery?
How to tell the holy tingle
from bad nerves and vacations long overdue.
A band of trespassing campers, fathers
with young sons, files from the margin
across the face some farmer must
have cleared, unless local lore
holds true, and the heart marks an absence,
a place burned over where nothing new grows.

Snow at Dodona

What do I know of how priests felt
asleep in the snow at Dodona,
dirty feet unwashed because the dirt

turned sacred the moment an Egyptian dove
settled in an oak there? What do I know
of serving an oracle, watching her twitch

like an epileptic, the wild lips
difficult to read and needing care
with sponge and salve after her fit?

Not much. But once I stood in ruins
smothered in new snow, Mount Tomaros
bending above, in the exorbitant glare

my eyes useless but my ears glued
to the only sound in the empty valley,
a wooden flute played by the only other

human at Dodona, her cold notes
encoding a loneliness unknown by even
stones on the moon, unless I failed

and misconstrued the fragile scales
unspooling a tune that sewed us closer
while red mud welled in my footprints like blood.

Painting the Boat

Scrape the chips, sand the blisters
down through old coats to
bare hull, smooth, vulnerable

to saltwater, rust, barnacles, Maine's
hungry coast. In May
her gunwales look fine but her hull

shows the tolls of last summer's landings,
exploratory nosings into island
coves, or low-tide ledges

bumped and grounded on. A fresh brush
slathers new layers over
transom, prow, curving

ribs (I refuse to
use a spray can), and other parts
of her no one sees

once she's in the water. For now
wind breaks on the keel which
cuts near-solstice sun leaving

a wake of shade. She'll finish drying
tonight in full moon. Locals hold
a blue boat bad luck but

this blue's no threat to a jealous
sea; it's the color of indigo
buntings splashing the pasture

back home in Virginia and besides
they claimed it bad luck when I married
you in the rain a year ago.

Blood and Snow

Born the thirteenth, he's thirteen
days old in a small house swaddled in
twenty-six inches of snow. Knee-deep
impasse, our packed road stands
as much chance of whisking him to town
as to another planet. The world outside
wallows in white whiter than milk
dribbling from his mother's nipples,
but the world outside still lies
beyond the power of his eyes.

Open, his eyes lick light from my face,
suck each feature slowly in turn
through the black of their pupils
back to a room, some insulated attic,
I'm now stacked within; closed, they jerk,
working his lids like burrowing moles
just below the nervous surface.

A slammed door, the dropped pan startle him,
arching his back, jarring his limbs,
yet he craves the flavor of voices.
His skin can't take the feel of space;
in nakedness he flails the air
with the same fear Adam felt. From his sleep
he laughs like a loon far across the lake.

Locked from town, he's wrapped on my lap.
His mother naps. Snow salts the sky
beyond the book propped by his head.
So much to read: the page, the storm,
his face twisted as in pain or rage.
Gas? A dream? Or the warm
smell of blood returning from his birth,
clots his mother lost that wouldn't stop
and could have cost him her?
Afterwards, they stripped the bed, mopped
the floor, sponged the walls, but who can know?
Maybe even all this snow
can't bleach that blood from where it dries
inside the world behind his eyes.

Rapunzel

I brush your hair
one hundred strokes
once the boy goes to bed.

You like stiff bristles; they coax
oils from your scalp that flare
in the candlelight, each thread

down your back so electric it looks
like the spoke of a nimbus you've bred
toward the ground. Long hair's too rare

these days, the copperhead
stunned in the road by the equinox
that combs from our air

all the winged things dispirited
by winter. But I'm going nowhere,
butterflies and hawks

migrating south; I'm through with solitaire.
Let me braid your hair instead.
Once from the shawl that cloaks

your shoulders I've wrapped a rope, a stair
to climb beyond the oldest oaks,
let it be my ladder up. I'm ready to be led.

Month-names lengthen with the lengthening night
like the hair of those buried. In the ring
a small boy on horseback holds out his arms
as though in flight, learning to trot
an old pony before dinner. Funny how
the darkening months can end in *ember*
and how through the sudden flooding of eyes
his black helmet bleeds into evening air
blackening everything. Arms out, legs tight,
he circles the ring, a fenced lozenge
of red dirt and dead grass where he can be
master of his small portion, his share
of light on a short day, casting his lot
like the tribes dicing for Canaan at Shiloh.

Just the End of Time

In a window-seat on a wing
I cross with the jetstream
against the grain of their sailing,

thirty-six Calvinists sea-sick four months,
their *Fortune* bucking the North Atlantic
eleven limbs up my family tree.

I'd rather go by boat,
even nauseous in a leaky one,
than claustrophobic in this airless cabin

six miles deep in night, pressurized
and piecing a puzzle with my son
above the graves of slaves.

We're loading Noah's ark,
squeezing in yellow elephants,
purple hippos, blue lions,

and last into red sky a raven
or black dove. Noah floated
one hundred fifty days; we fly

six hours, another five
wolfed by voracious space.
Is this what Einstein meant?

Where do those hours hide
or the twenty years
ago today a New York farm

aped Gardner's shots of Maryland cornfields
without the dead, as survivors woke
to Hendrix and Key's anthem

that muddy Monday dawn,
its anniversary oozing
beyond my flashing wing-tip?

The Kingdom of Things

When the heart valve buckles
or the brain vessel ruptures and I,
at last accomplished, stumble sloshed
in blood over the edge of the earth
into the faulty recall of a few people,
don't weep for me.

Where I'm going there's no warranty;
no estimates, parts, labor; no car
in the shop, stove on the fritz, fridge
on the blink; no days waiting for
angels to flap out and chant the good news
I need a new furnace.

In paradise they had to prune and lop
the overgrowing brush and branches,
which doesn't sound like paradise to me
as much as a land that's honeysuckle-free
where houses stay painted, shingles uncurled,
dirt roads graded and graveled;

but thanks to paradise the only things
that need no maintenance have passed
away into perfection, which means to wish
to do no maintenance is to wish to pass away
from my dilapidated castle, from her
I wrestled through delivery

of him we brought home years ago
today, and from the mess they've made
of my resolve to fall for nothing
and no one
about to break, breaking, or broken.

I have a son; I want a daughter.
My conscience says it ought to matter
only that the child be whole.
But what does conscience know?
It's nothing but the voice of parents
stenciled deep inside, and mine
got one of each, so why should I
trust them? On the screen the shapes
of limbs and organs wait to be
identified: head, heart, spine
I recognize, yet have to take on faith
a face the nurse points out to me.
But what's the sex? The ultrasonic
scanner zeroes in, and there it is,
the likeness of a fist and middle
finger flipped at me saying Forget
your ideas of symmetry and balance,
not to mention men and women.
Good-bye, daughter; hello, son.
No loss has made me laugh so long.

He could be clearing a minefield,
sweeping the detector's silver shaft
from side to side in slow arcs,
then stepping carefully after
like an underage boy come home drunk
to the angry sleep of his fragile parents.

But he's only clearing weeds,
equipped with plastic goggles, surgical mask,
and monstrous ear-muffs that cushion his drums
against the pummeling gas-powered decibels.

He's not much for growing;
that's his wife's department.
But mowing, pruning, and this chore
he performs with sufficient skill to afford himself
a certain pleasure, if not joy,
and their arrangement flourishes.

There's nothing grim about his reaping.
Around the log-bridge where his young sons play
he shaves the snake-concealing grass yet leaves
one flowering weed his older boy admires,
a yellow head of tangled hair
the labor-saving scythe has spared.

But this labor tires, too.
The machine darts shards of twigs and vines
which fix in his pants like quills.
Vibration saps his arms.
The goggles fill with sweat,
as does the mask with sneezes

fierce enough to drive him inside,
report his progress, and shower before lunch,
but she runs from the house to return in tears,
shaking a fistful of expensive lilies
he dimly recalls through the fog of his goggles.

How was he to know
the last time he brought her flowers
the next time it would be this bad, unbloomed bouquet?
Through a sullen lunch he smarts with the misstep,
with his failure to identify, with the sudden
detonation that blows their hearts apart.

Adoration

I ask nothing but to enjoy the presence
of what's present. Why is this so hard?
To savor the crickets makes better sense
than moping that summer has quit our yard.
Why hear the crickets purr and feel the creak
of September's bones or mind that this year
blows cicadas away? Why even speak
of what's passed to our sister hemisphere?

Here at hand float the bodies of two boys
adrift in a bay of dreams, here the lithe
body of one tried by the curse on Eve.
Flinching in fear of what I'll lose destroys.
Poise is my work; let me, if not believe,
adore the toil, bless the sweat, kiss the scythe.

But for the laundry Nausikaa would never
have found him naked, skin inflamed by salt
as by excruciating eczema.
But for her soiled silks she'd never have come
where green sea nibbles the splintered cliffs
to wash the intimations of her body
from delicate fabrics into fresh creek
streaming over amber sand or led him,
bathed and clothed, through groves of lemons
back to the palace, famished for his foreign
stories, the kingdoms, monsters, nymphs
one strains hard to glimpse or hear,
wringing out a spouse's socks, a child's underwear.

He has never heard of Thebes or the Sphinx.
Having never solved a riddle, he thinks
throwing a towel around his shoulders
makes him a king. He couldn't care less
about crossroads or plagues and without shame
chooses for queen that exquisite princess,
his mother. When I hug her, he screams
Leave my girl alone, from my point of view
an improvement over the son who wedged
between us in the bed and commanded
Daddy, you go die. How long can I stand
to play the villain healthy sons must hate
for Viennese oracles to be fulfilled?
In their sweetest dreaming I get killed

as the dreams I brewed deep in the cave
of preschool sleep, curled up with hippo
or woolly goat, killed the man who beat me
to the sheets I never shared. Afternoons
we horsed around in cartoon combat,
I Popeye, he Brutus, while in all our scenes
Olive Oyl clung to the couch and invoked
the potent magic canned in spinach greens.
My Brutus knew his part, taking the fall,
but how does a father know when to give
his son the taste of winning, the flavor
of total victory if total victory
means catastrophe for the boy it leaves
a blinded old man led by the hand?

Blue Pajamas

I perform the offices of comfort
as best I can. My wife away,
he moans through the corridor
at four in the morning, *Lie down with me,*
I'm lonely. In this matter, I know I am
his second choice, my face a face
no razor makes a mother's, my breath
always a father's breath.
Still, I lie down with the lamb
he sleeps with again, now that he knows
a second baby's coming, and wait
for the short, shallow intakes of air
to deepen their draw
through the well of his belly.

I put it all on the line
one piece at a time. The sun not up,
wet laundry stings my hands, stiffening
the fingers that squeeze open clothespins
as though I'd suffered a stroke. *Will you die?*
he asks over breakfast. *If you and Mommy die,*
I'll be lonely. In the wind
his sleepsuit flicks its members
faster than in tantrums, fluttering
jay-blue cotton against the Judas trees
that lathered pink last week. At bedtime
the cotton smells purged of his body
folded on my lap. *Lie down with me,*
he whispers. In the dark
after the book
I kiss my final kiss.

Notes

"Except I Shall See": John 20:25 (King James Version). During the winter of 1863-1864, Robert E. Lee worshiped at St. Thomas Episcopal Church, Orange, Virginia.

"'War, Effect of a Shell on a Confederate Soldier'": The photographs and details about Gardner appear in William A. Frassanito's *Gettysburg: A Journey in Time* (New York: Scribner's, 1975).

"Invidia": From *The Seven Deadly Sins,* a series of engravings executed by Jacob Matham and based on drawings by Hendrick Goltzius.

"The Loveliest Beach in the World," "Old Perithia": Both on the island of Corfu, Greece. "Almighty" translates *Pantokrator,* name of the highest mountain on the island.

"The Death Oracle at Ephyra": Near Parga in Epiros, Greece, and reputedly the site of Odysseus's visit to the underworld.